Gazing at the Lighthouse

❦

Reflections on the Loving Life

N. Michael Murphy, MD

Trio Books

ISBN-10: 0-9845966-2-3
EAN-13: 978-0-9845966-2-1
Library of Congress Control Number: 2010909049

Cover design © John Carlson
With love and gratitude I give thanks to the lighthouse and to the Soul and Spirit of the Beara Peninsula that encouraged me to be and to become. Thanks to all the Mortals whose love and inspirational lives moved me to exhale these words, with especial thanks to John Carlson. Thanks also to those who read what appeared on paper and gave me gentle editorial nudges, especially Tim Cahill.

To the Soul and Spirit of Beara
and to the beautiful Mortals who live there
and are dying to talk about it.
And to my roots,
especially my father Bernard Murphy
who was at a loss for words

Contents

Foreword

For the past several years, my father has lived in the village of Castletownbere in Ireland, where his father was born in 1888. The lovely cottage in which he lives looks out on the usually misty, frequently tempestuous, always breathtaking expanse of the Atlantic Ocean. In the foreground of that vista lies the western end of Bere Island, with its 1850-vintage lighthouse that guides boats to safe harbor in Castletownbere.

Offering a steady, silent, welcoming light, that lighthouse became an ever-present metaphor for the healing power of the steady, silent, unconditionally loving gaze, a power so often manifested during Michael's workshops in Love, Loss, and Forgiveness. Held in an astonishingly beautiful setting not far from his cottage—the Buddhist retreat center of Dzogchen Beara, perched on a cliff overlooking the Atlantic—these workshops nurtured equally astonishing transformations among participants.

The gaze lay at the heart of these transformations, as I experienced for myself while taking part in two of those workshops. So simple in form, so easy to forget, so necessary to practice, the loving gaze—at oneself first and then at others—provides safe harbor for the Mortal to reencounter Soul and Spirit and bask in the healing of that reconnection.

In his workshops, my father draws upon a sea-based metaphor. In it, the moist, receptive sea is the Soul and the vast, windswept sky is the Spirit. At the interface of sea and sky, the tiny boat that is the Mortal floats. Buoyed by the Soul's deep waters and propelled by the inspiring winds of the Spirit, the Mortal embarks on a lifelong journey of love.

Sitting in his often rainswept sunroom, gazing out on the Bere Island lighthouse, my father distilled the unveilings and transformations he has witnessed so many times in his workshops into the *pensées* in this collection. These meditations serve as gentle reminders—nudges, as my father would say—to let go of burdens and step into the grace of living a life of unconditional love.

Alexandra Murphy
Flagstaff,
Arizona

A Trinitarian Myth of Love and Remembrance

The Soul and the Spirit came from far upriver.
They swirled and twirled downstream into a woman by way of a man
and joined the Mortal child in his mother's womb.
Soon the child was born, entering the world complete and perfect
in his three natures—Mortal, Soul, and Spirit.
The child gazed at his mother and she gazed at him, and they became
"in" love.
The father gazed at his child and his child gazed at him, and they too
became in love
and the child sang a song: "May I never forget who I am and where I
came from."
As the child grew, his parents feared for his Mortality and his fragility
and they spent many years strengthening his outer Mortal shell.
They thickened his skin and adorned him with titles and treasures
while filling his mind with ingredients for success, so that he became
famous and strong,
but the song of the child became a lament: "I have already forgotten."
No longer did he feel the loving warmth and joy from Soul and Spirit,
for they were muffled by the thickness of his shell,
 and in losing sight of his Soul and Spirit, he forgot about love.
On awakening from his dreams of immortality, the Mortal realized that
he must let go
of fame and fortune to make a place for all three members of his nature
and become whole once more,
for he knew that he would only be in love again
when he remembered who he was and where he came from.

The Gaze and The Look

The Gaze is far-sighted, and an all-embracing act of lovers. The gaze is a soft and profound manifestation of unconditional love. The gaze is about loving the child and the adolescent and the adult and the old-person-in-waiting within who scream silently or loudly for our appreciation. The gaze is about cherishing the fragile Mortal who may make dreadful mistakes. Errors and betrayals accompanied by guilt and shame are often carried as weighty burdens by Mortals who do not know how to let them go. The gaze dissolves all guilt and bathes the Mortal in smiles so that he may live and laugh and cry and die in love. The gaze warms and enlivens the Mortal who craves to give and receive love and yet is so apt to dispense meanness and cruelty.

The Look is a brief inspection or perhaps a more detailed inventory made by inquisitors. Looking is hard and analytical and judgment-prone, and staring is a magnification of looking when we are unable or unwilling to let go and move on. We may "look into it" and follow up with "evidence" and even a trial of one kind or another, but how can we possibly know? We look and judge from outer consciousness and outer awareness, and yet we feel and are moved from our inner being that may be—and usually is—some distance from our consciousness and awareness.

Who is to judge? We are the first in a long line of judges of ourselves, and our self- esteem is often bruised and battered by our harsh verdicts and by our outlook.

We may treasure our looks, but we need our gaze.

Love for a Child

We gaze at a child, and we fall in love. We fall in love because right before our eyes is a manifestation of unconditional love. A welcoming moist Soul greets us and draws us in, and an exuberant wild Spirit kicks and waves with the joy of life, and all this energy is wrapped in a fragile-appearing Mortal whose bodily functions are plain to see and hear and smell. This beautiful apparition is unconditional love personified, and all of us wish to know unconditional love.

Narcissus looked and looked into the reflecting pool and all he saw after eons of looking was a beautiful Mortal image but no Soul and Spirit and he despaired, for he knew that without Soul and Spirit he would never be in love. A few Mortals who, like Narcissus, are unable to gaze and so are unable to discover their Soul and their Spirit may seek to steal Soul and Spirit from another. Knowing that he is incomplete—just as Narcissus knew about his deficiency before committing suicide—the pedophile attempts to steal what is missing in himself from a child, and in so doing commits Soul murder.

When a child is Soul-murdered, the abused child-become-adult needs to remember his Soul and Spirit by gazing with endless love and compassion deep into the mirror at his lost child. In this way, the child becomes reunited with Soul and Spirit and is then able to live his life in love. Imprisoning the narcissistic pedophile, or seeking financial compensation, or endlessly talking about the abuse is of no help to the Soul-murdered Mortal. Only remembering and gazing and loving will restore his perfection.

To Be and to Become

To breathe
and watch the breath
is to be aware of living and being.

To be with the breath
is to be a mortal, being;
to lose awareness of the breath
is to be a mortal, doing.

To gaze in the mirror with loving compassion
is to become more than the sum of the parts
for gazing is becoming,
and when I gaze at another
we become more than we were.

We need the breath and the gaze
to be creatively and becomingly alive,
for then we are pregnant
with a life of endless possibilities.

Awakening

In the waking dream that was my life, there was little room for doubt
or urge to stem the endless flow of words that heralded my being.
Now the dream is over.
Awake, I need someone to believe in,
so from this moment on I will believe in myself.
With my Soul and my Spirit I will gaze into the mirror
and embrace my Mortal nature,
for only then will I be sure that there is someone
who believes in me.

Belonging

*"If you bring forth that which is in you,
that which is in you will save you.
If you do not bring forth that which is within you,
that which is in you will destroy you."*
Didymos Judas Thomas

Early one morning I was pondering the next workshop I was to facilitate for the Love, Loss, and Forgiveness Project and realized that of recent years the workshops have become like lighthouses: aids to navigation that illuminate the rock-strewn inlets in my life. When I am within the luminous circle of such a lighthouse, I feel safe, for I know I belong.

Belonging: longing to be, and not feeling obliged to do or to perform. Longing to be heard, and longing for my reflection to be seen and acknowledged and loved by others, for only then am I sure that I exist as more than part of the belongings of myself or others. "Belongings" are part of the external world—part of outer consciousness or outer awareness. But to belong is to be in touch with what lies within.

What lies within is love. Intimacy is an invitation to others to "into-me-see" and share love. Most of the time—out of range of the lighthouse—we are afraid of gazing within or allowing others to gaze into us, for fear that something monstrous like Original Sin lives there that does not bear knowing. So we cover up with powder and paint and pomp and circumstance, and we may never really get to know ourselves or ever feel that we belong.

But I long for into-me-see, and I am so privileged to see into you, for it is then, in that place within, that I am "in" love and my life has the clearest meaning. In these workshop lighthouses, we always use the

Talking Stick when we first meet in the circle of light, for it weaves a delicate gossamer of well-being around us in which we will be seen and heard and loved, and it only takes a round or two of the Talking Stick for each of us to remember that we belong. Later, in our practices in trios, we experience deep aspects of love, of loss, and of forgiveness, and realize that loss is a powerful teacher about love and forgiveness.

These moments in trios are intimate, because we feel empowered to allow the two others in the trio to into-me-see. We allow them into our inner sanctum, which we usually keep hidden, and discover that they are not appalled as we imagined they would be, for they love what they gaze at and feel. They love me, and I am able to see that love through their reflection, and this reflection makes me better prepared to love myself.

What magic! What a recipe for loving and for living! Yet we need to continue to revisit the lighthouse throughout our lives, and we need to refine and practice the loving life so that it becomes part of us. Then we will be able to use these gourmet inner recipes for living to nourish our everyday lives, for that which is within us will save us.

What happens at the lighthouse is almost beyond words, and our partner as well as our children and friends may find it difficult to understand when we return home. But they will notice the effect when we love ourselves more and know that we belong, and perhaps one day they will join us at the lighthouse.

Gazing with E. F. Schumacher

Ernst Friedrich Schumacher was born in Bonn, Germany, in 1911, spent a few important years in early adulthood in the United States, and then lived most of his adult life in England. There he became chief economic advisor to the National Coal Board, as well as a wise voice during years of war and the years of malignant growth and consumption that followed. A marvelous intellect and great wit, he was the most interesting of speakers, but the inner world of feelings was not easy for him until he met Muschi, who became his wife. She was in awe of his mind and showered him with tenderness and warmth that prepared him for intimacy.

It was some years later, after he spent time in Burma, that Schumacher developed what he called "Buddhist Economics," which stated that the purpose of nations was to provide work in which people were able to use their innate skills collaboratively to provide for a "becoming" existence. Economic progress, he said, should go as far as sufficiency but no further, since it would foster greed, evil, and a waste of resources. With sufficiency, we would employ "appropriate technology" and not tolerate the malignant growth of technology that has taken over our lives.

In his book *A Guide for the Perplexed,* Schumacher suggested that there are four levels of being: Mineral, Plant, Animal, and Man. The distinguishing difference between mineral and plant is *life*, which we can recognize and destroy but not create. Between plant and animal there is *consciousness,* which we can also recognize and eliminate but know little about, and animals also exhibit some degree of thought and intelligence. Between the level of animal and man there is *self-consciousness* and *self-awareness*, but this power (of intimacy) is an unlimited potentiality rather than an actuality. I imagine that when Mortal man is in touch with his center—with his Soul and Spirit—he has unlimited potential, and the unlimited potential is love.

Schumacher said that the whole man—a Mortal in touch with Soul and Spirit, as I imagine it—may know something about the mineral world, but not a lot about the plant and animal worlds. Yet if he is self-aware, he will truly be in touch with the center and be familiar with intimacy—with himself and with others and with nature.

Schumacher uses this perspective to contrast with the materialistic scientific point of view, which argues that what is "real" is inanimate matter, yet science has difficulty in defining life, consciousness, and self-awareness despite the fact all individuals can verify those phenomena from their own experience. I believe that "scientific" allopathic medicine knows a fair amount about the mineral level—the building blocks of man—but little about both life and consciousness and less still about self-awareness. So the science of medicine treats man as being at the upper end of the animal, or third, level of being, since it is unable to measure or even recognize the fourth level of self-awareness. Thus intimacy or Soul and Spirit has little place in the teaching or practice of allopathic medicine, and this makes it woefully inadequate in the healing of man.

The gaze is an opening into self-awareness and an invitation to the unlimited potential of love. If more of us lived our lives in this state of being, with sufficiency as our collective aim and collaboration rather than competition as our way, our unlimited potential would ensure that both our life and our death are lived in love.

Loving Intimacy

When I gaze-into-me, it becomes possible to love myself unconditionally and not depend on *you* to be the love in my life. Only when I love myself unconditionally am I free and able to invite you to "into-me-see," and if you enter, we become "in" love together. The mutual gaze that accompanies shared intimacy is the affirmation of love, and through this reflection I know for sure that I exist.

The Perfect Stranger

Imagine that we encounter ourselves as a perfect stranger! What would we say? "How are you?" Then what? We may quickly exhaust the stock phrases, look at our watch, say that we are late, and ask ourselves to have a good day, whatever that means.

If we are to see the perfection in our-self-the-stranger, we need intimacy. Not "intimate" as with a leer or an ogle or a thinly disguised sexual request to let me into you, for that is a power push that has nothing to do with love or the kind of intimacy we crave. The intimacy we need can occur by giving my self a soft and loving gaze in the mirror, the portal to my inner being. As I gaze, the one in the mirror gazes back at me and opens the gate into his inner self; he invites into-me-see, proposing that we have all the time in the world and beyond to tell about fears and worries and screams that will melt away in this loving incubator of love. In my inner being, the stranger vanishes, and only perfection remains.

But if I my Mortal nature is to be intimate, I need more time for myself and not be in such a rush to flee to important appointments, with an empty aside to "have a good day."

The Dining Table

Where has it gone? She told us that there was once a dining room in which all her family ate together at the appointed time. The dining table was round, so there was no head and all were seen. "My parents and the four children," she said, "were the regular cast, with occasional assorted relatives and a regular supply of interesting guests as extras. When the family was alone, my brothers verbally competed for center stage, with father acting as a benign and rather unobtrusive director, and mother and I were the audience, who usually relished being witnesses of the play.

The dining room was a sacred place for nourishment of all kinds where I received holy and sometimes unholy communion, with words upon words that built my foundation cemented with love. With the years, the details have mostly vanished, but those words and feelings of togetherness remain like rocks sculpted by the winds and the rain. In this safe setting, my inner being took root, and I would not be as I am without it."

Now the dining room is barely used, since fast food and sound bytes take up so little space. The table is often scattered with papers and magazines and perhaps a computer or two, but people seldom sit there together for very long. Perhaps nothing much is sacred anymore and our Souls and Spirits have retreated into cyberspace because we Mortals have too little time for them.

There is hunger at many empty tables that fast food and riches will not fill.

Being At Home

The essence of being at home is contained within the words "Glad to See You!" If on waking, I gaze for a few moments in the mirror and say, "Glad to See You!" I am at home. If I am glad to see me, then those same words spoken by you magnify my sense of belonging, and I am also at home with you. If I ignore me, then your "Glad to See You" may evoke a response like "Yes, but if you only knew!" as if Knowing has anything at all to do with Loving and being Glad!

Coffee

In a sun-drenched Parisian café, I sit drinking coffee and gaze at the passersby. My inner being is filled with gladness and content. Babbling French chatter adds music to the morning air that rises like mist from the river Seine and all is well. Yet sometimes, when dark clouds gather within, gloomy feelings let loose an avalanche of chatter and fears from my troubled mind, and I am unable to sit still. With this fit of restlessness, I might rise up, pay the bill, and leave, forgetting that these dark forebodings when gazed at with a smile and with a sip of coffee become transformed into love and even more love, and I can settle down.

Imaginary People

Jorges Luis Borges wrote a powerful short story about imagining immortality. *The Circular Ruins* is a tale about a wizard whose task it was to go down to the ruins of a temple on a riverbank and dream up a son. For three years he lay in the temple, fed and watched over by fearful natives. Eventually the son of his dreams was complete in every detail except that he had no life. Fire visited the wizard and promised that he would breathe life into the son if the wizard would tell no one. With the breath of Fire the son became alive, but the wizard was afraid that his son would discover his origins: *"Not to be a man, to be a projection of another man's dreams—what an incomparable humiliation, what madness!"*

When the wizard became old and was about to die, Fire came once more. The wizard walked up to Fire, but it did not harm him. It was at that moment the wizard realized that he, too, was the dream of someone's imagination.

I often wonder how many of us are the dream of a parent's imagination or denial or fear of mortality, and how many children dream up their parents? What humiliation! What madness! Oh that we would know and love ourselves and each other intimately and not as bit parts in a living dream!

The Illusion of Knowing

Looking at people when we meet, we often use their first names, sometimes as a deception meant to reassure. Perhaps in our loneliness we add them to the list of people we imagine that we "know," or we might even promote them to "friend" in a Facebook account.

Looks and casual glances simply bounce off polished exteriors. People seldom meet intimately even when they are in close proximity, and these other-brushings leave us with only conjectures or shadows created by our imagination.

What impressions or pictures do I present to others? Whatever they are, I know that the impersonation is only more or less me. I give different signals, especially when I am more than usually unsure of who I am. Maybe I want them to be impressed—with what, I wonder? That I am bigger and more important and wiser than either they or I imagine? That I am attractive, with the impossible promise of intellectual, sexual, or financial powers that are far beyond me?

Looks and impressions, often created along with the command to "smile," seldom reflect what lies behind the role of the moment. If we have never gazed, we may imagine that there is nothing much of value within our inner being, or that our inner world contains only darkness and secrets and buried skeletons from which we and others flee.

What if there was no judgment? What if everyone and everything that we gazed at were seen as treasures that with a touch of alchemy became love, and that there was no need for masks and illusions?

The Present Past

We are unable to move on from the past if it is still present. The past will only move on and merge with the present when it is gazed at with love. We need not forget the past, nor should we, because it is part of our present fabric. But if it is heavy and painful, and its presence is a constant irritation in the present moment, we need the gaze that will soften it so that it can take its rightful place.

Through the Looking-Glass

We want so many things from the treasure house in which we live our lives, but all we need is love. When I Googled the word "need," in 0.78 seconds I was offered 1,280,000,000 results from the query, suggesting perhaps that our needs are endless and could not be addressed in a lifetime. I consulted Humpty Dumpty in Wonderland about the 1.28 billion references to the word "need", and I think he shed some light: *"When I use a word," Humpty Dumpty said in rather a scornful tone, "it means just what I choose it to mean—neither more nor less."**

If the infant could speak, she would tell us that the one thing she needs is love. She knows how to gurgle if not Google, and the only word for her gurgle is love. The trouble begins when all those Mortals around her act as though they are experts on the subject of need and start to fill her mind with just a few of the 1.28 billion contributions on the subject. It is then that she forgets what she knew and begins her endless search to become someone else and find what others say she needs.

She is led to believe that somewhere "out there" in virtual reality is the answer. It must be in education or art or science or religion or politics or genetics or psychology or medicine or advertising or shopping— so much to learn (only 1.28 billion more to go). Harried and stressed, and feeling overwhelmed and inadequate and unfulfilled, she glances in the mirror. With a gasp, she quickly turns away from what she sees, and readjusts her mask before continuing her quest. "What I need and am looking for can't possibly be in the looking-glass," she says, but it is.

---

*   Lewis Carroll, *Through the Looking-Glass*, chapter 6

Gazing with Edvard Munch

Edvard Munch, a film by Peter Watkins, vividly portrays the life and work of the artist who painted as no one else the pain, loneliness, and terror he observed from deep within his ever-present past.

Edvard Munch was born on December 12, 1863, in Loton, Norway, the second child of five. A year after he was born the family moved to Kristiania (later renamed Oslo), and his mother died there of tuberculosis in 1868. The family was devastated, but Edvard received some solace from the close relationship he had with his sister Sophie, who was one year older. Nine years after mother's death, Sophie also died of tuberculosis, at the age of fifteen.

When he was seventeen, Munch decided to become an artist, enrolling in the Royal School of Drawing in Kristiania in 1881, and from then on he struggled to express on canvas what he experienced within his inner being. In 1886, a few months before the death of his long-depressed physician father, Munch painted several versions of *The Sick Child*, inspired by Sophie's death, and this breathtaking painting seems like a wail that made his grief visible, and was prelude to *The Scream*, which had been gestating in him for many years.

As one gazes at Munch's many self-portraits, the screams of his life seem barely hidden beneath the surface, even though he usually imagined himself as others saw him in everyday life: well-disguised in tailored suits and gloves, as befitted his station. In 1892 he painted *Despair*, and in 1893 he brought the despairing *Scream* into the light. The completion of this masterpiece about the inner world of the grieving and lost child-adolescent-adult was further marked by two more family tragedies. First his younger sister developed schizophrenia, and then in 1895 his brother Andreas died.

In Munch's most famous work, I noticed that the screamer has turned his back on the two companions accompanying him on his walk. The screamer became out of touch with his Soul and his Spirit, and they are a distance away. His Mortal self is alone, without the loving consolation that intimacy with his Soul and Spirit would have provided. *The Scream* grips most of us who witness it, for we have all screamed silent or not-so-silent screams many times throughout our lives. Our screams, like those of Munch, will only be softened and lose their intensity if we gaze at them with the love of our Soul and Spirit.

For Munch, his screams were never softened by his loving gaze. Like any child, he looked to his mother for the gaze he needed to provide himself with a loving foundation, for as children we need the loving gaze from parents in order to learn how to give love to ourselves and others. After mother's death, Munch continued to receive love from Sophie and perhaps from others, but Sophie died in childhood, and *The Scream* was his terrified and lonely response to his losses and self-doubt. As an adult, he continued to seek the feminine loving gaze from women, but romantic love could never give him the loving foundation that only he himself could provide. So his relationships with women were disastrous, and his ambivalence was never better illustrated than in *The Vampire,* initially entitled *Love and Pain.*

While his art must have offered more relief from his distress than his alcoholism, and given him the energy and Spirit to continue living, Munch lived a reclusive life despite fame and fortune in later years. Even the *Self-Portrait: Between Clock and Bed,* painted two years before his death on January 23, 1944, shows his lifelong loneliness and the imprinted scream on his face.

No artist has ever portrayed the inner darkness and terrors of grief, loneliness, and despair more vividly than Munch, but he was unable to gaze through and beyond those horrors into Love that awaited him within.

Fiction

*"The stories other people tell about you
and the stories you tell about yourself:
which come closer to the truth?"*
Prado, in Pascal Mercier's *Night Train to Lisbon*

If our inner being is closed to others and even to ourselves, we can only speak the truth (or falsehoods) about outer awareness, and in outer awareness, with all its make-believe, I often wonder who comes closer to the truth!

But in our inner being—in the realm of Soul and Spirit—true and false have no place, for in the ebb and flow of Soul and Spirit, changes occur from moment to moment. When I am gazing at you with love, I become you, or at least I become more than me, and the same is also true when I gaze at nature.

If we ask the question "Who am I?" from our outer awareness or outer being, the answer might well be, "Your guess is as good as mine." If we ask the same question from the place of unconditional love in our inner being, the answer would simply be "Love" or else "Everything!"

The Wishing Well

I used to think that if I had done things differently earlier in my life, or if my parents had loved themselves so that they were better prepared to love me, all would have been well.

But I am marked by events just as a canvas is marked by brush-strokes, and if my earlier life had been different, this masterpiece would not exist!

What Do We Mean?

Our fearful mind uses denial to turn away from death, and the confrontational words of Thornton Wilder in the last paragraph of *The Bridge of San Luis Rey** may startle and frighten us. *"Soon we shall die,"* he said, *"and we ourselves shall be loved for a while and forgotten."* Unbelievable and unacceptable, and yet life *is* very short, and all memory of our being *will* be forgotten in a generation or two, if not earlier. "Oh no!" we cry, "I will never forget you," but we do.

And Wilder concludes: *"There is a land of the living and a land of the dead and the bridge is love, the only survival, the only meaning."* The bridge between life and death is the deep and everlasting loving gaze that is the only real meaning of our existence, for in the gaze, we discover or rediscover love. If we never love ourselves or others—if we are out of touch with our Soul and Spirit and never gaze at life and death—life becomes meaningless and nothing survives.

* Thornton Wilder, *The Bridge of San Luis Rey* (New York: Harper Collins reissue, 2004)

Moisture for the Soul

Without the life-giving element of water we are dust, yet much of what passes as care takes place in climate-controlled atmospheres that are deadly dry, devoid of the feminine healing moisture that springs from the tears and laughter and love of Mortals.

The feminine art of caregiving is of its nature moist, and we all need her lubrication if we are not to dry up and become dust, a state that may arise from the inner or outer droughts of our times. Tears are a solution. If we will cry a handful of tears, the tears may become the suspension into which we stir our grief so that we will not choke from the dust that comes of tears unshed.

If we are caregivers of any kind, we need not fear crying (or laughing till we cry) with the one for whom we care, since the tears are simply moisture that provides cleansing and bestows blessings.

One little boy I met in the hospice insisted on putting his tear-stained tissue into his grandfather's casket at the wake, for he knew that his tears of love were an eternal remedy.

Loneliness

Loneliness is an extended silent scream. It is the state of feeling abandoned by Soul so that the Mortal feels absolutely alone, even when there are people around voicing volumes of reassuring words. Soul may fade away in childhood if the young Mortal is subjected to physical or sexual abuse or if the child is unloved and neglected. Soul can disappear when the Mortal experiences terror and fear of death in wars on the battlefield or skirmishes in the marketplace. Burnout and Post Traumatic Soul Disaster are the result of experiencing the absence of the loving, witnessing Soul, without which life feels meaningless.

Loneliness will only respond to the gaze, for it is the gaze that revives the Mortal through the breath of life and love. It helps a little when others gaze at us, but the healing of loneliness will only occur when we gaze at ourselves with love and compassion.

Let's Get Married

When we marry, we promise to love and care for our partner through good times and bad, but make no promise that we will love and take care of ourselves. Many who marry don't love themselves very much and neglect their own self-care, hoping that their partner will provide the love they need. But we are unable to provide durable self-awareness and self-esteem for anyone but ourself. So one or both in the couple may become disappointed about the imagined failure of the partner when the passion of romantic love has ebbed, and look for another who, we imagine, will be more forthcoming.

If we take the responsibility of marrying ourselves before asking another to marry us, we will be better prepared for our marriage to another. When we marry ourselves, we promise to love and cherish our three natures till death do us part. We promise to cherish our Mortal nature that lives and ages and dies. We promise to love our feminine or Soul nature that loves unconditionally, and our masculine or Spirit nature that provides guidance and enthusiasm for living the loving life.

Loving and taking care of ourselves is so very simple, but since we have never been taught about its importance, it is very rarely done! A good way of doing it is to *gaze* softly and lovingly in the mirror every morning (and more often) at our Mortal reflection without any criticism or judgment. The gazer is our Soul and our Spirit, welcoming the often fragile and stressed Mortal to the new day, saying "I love you!" *and meaning it.*

So let's marry ourselves as a graduation present when we leave school, affirming that we are going to live life lovingly. As a wedding present to ourselves, a beautiful mirror, for when we marry ourselves we need to gaze lovingly every day in the mirror as a daily remembrance of our vows!

A Puff of Wind

Our childhood screams
need our gaze
together with a gentle puff of warmed breath
to send them on their way,
for the gaze and the breath
will transform those gasps of suffering
into energy for the loving life.

Post Traumatic Soul Destruction

We make killing machines out of so many of our soldiers. If we are patriotic, we are supposed to admire and support the barking and yelling and abuse of the drill sergeants, and ignore the loss of warmth and softness in these beautiful young recruits who attempt to defend our country and spread democracy, often at the expense of loss of Soul. Sometimes there seems to be very little difference between the killing machines we create and the suicide bomber killing machines that oppose them.

Warriors in commerce and the industrial world are also often dedicated to making killings and taking over the territory of others, and the cost to so many of them and those they touch is Soul destruction.

It is impossible to live and love as killing machines filled with fear and hatred, and those young soldiers whose Souls have been shattered are often overwhelmed by loneliness on their return to the security of the homeland, since they have lost touch with their inner lives wherein lies love and compassion.

Relationships fall apart because of the absence of love, and some of the returning warriors will resort to addictive practices to fill the emptiness and loneliness. They become addicted to sex or alcohol or prescription and street drugs, but these addictions do not revive the Soul. Suicide is a natural urge when Soul is lost, as it was with Narcissus, and the post-traumatic effects of Soul Destruction lead to lives that are dreadfully hard to live.

The good news is that when these battered and abused Souls learn to gaze at themselves with compassion and freedom from judgment, the Soul is able to revive, for the practice of gazing will heal posttraumatic Soul destruction and burnout by resuscitating love.

Suicide

I have never been as cold as when I stood with a few others in the driving snow around the small hole into which we would bury his ashes. Nature could not have provided a more appropriate setting for the occasion.

I imagined him sending a last desperate message as a gift to all of us: "Love yourselves, for that is the only way to live."

The Mortal—you or me or anyone at all—without inner warmth cannot survive. We can try as parents or teachers or caregivers to give warmth to others, but if the fire of love and the warmth of witness and the gaze of Soul is absent from our life, we will eventually freeze to death.

I felt the inner coldness yesterday at the graveside, and I have felt it at times of self-loathing and despair, when no amount of Mortal distractions could warm my frigid Soul and Spirit.

"Take *real* care and gaze," he would have wished to say, "and do it *now*."

A Word for the Wise

If we are to come to light—if we are to gaze and touch and feel and be—we need the word, in order to express a sense of ourselves and each other and the nature of our surroundings. But words are used mostly for descriptions of outer awareness.

We attempt to explain ourselves and each other from the realm of outer consciousness and say who we think we are—or appear to be—and where we came from. But there are never enough words in this domain, and we will always be misunderstood by both ourselves and others.

The explanation and the meaning of our lives dwell in inner consciousness and not in appearances and in books and in wise saws and instances. Poetry may help, because it trims words to their essence:

in the beginning was the word
and the word was love
and the word became Mortal flesh
and blessed is the Mortal
whose parents love themselves and each other
for he is born in love as it was in the beginning.

Gazing with Samuel Beckett

Gazing at ourselves in the mirror is an exercise in self-awareness and an overture to love. The gaze is not the instinctive "look," which is usually an inspection of our outer being to determine whether or not our persona is in place and that we are suitably masked for public appearance. Gazing is a much more gentle action that caresses our inner world. Judgment has no place, for the gaze is an offering of love that is given as if we have all the time in the world till death do us part. Very simple, but not easy.

It was said that much of Beckett's work was drawn from his inner world: he looked within and put into words what he saw. For the most part, he seemingly perceived nothingness, meaninglessness, or farcical chaos, with but the briefest reference to love, as in *Krapp's Last Tape*.

I imagine *Waiting for Godot* to be a glimpse into the bleak inner lives of four men whose characters are all variations on the theme of self-disgust. What is chillingly apparent in that play is the absence of the feminine Soul in each of the men: Soul that would bring hope and love and warmth into their lives where there was none. I believe that the Godot that each one waits for is his or her own feminine nature—the Soul, without which one is incomplete—and we usually have no idea that this feminine nature is only a gaze away.

Happy Days is another tragicomedy, but here the tragedy is the absence of the masculine Spirit that would give Winnie the courage and energy to escape from the life-sapping trap she is in. Willie, her husband, is in the background, but he too lacks the courage to live. Beckett has said that Winnie's words "Nothing is funnier than unhappiness" were the most important in the play. It is certainly odd that many men and women unhappily wait for their feminine and their masculine natures—their Soul and their Spirit—to lift their Mortal selves out of the meaningless farce they have made of their lives. Such lives are indeed living examples in the theater of the absurd, about which Beckett is a master narrator.

In *"Endgame,"* the blind Hamm and Clov are intertwined in dependency and, like Estragon and Vladimir in *Waiting for Godot,* are unable to live with or without one another. *Endgame* is about beginnings and endings, but for Hamm and Clov, the loving life never begins and the lived life ("grain by grain") never ends. So they go through absurd routines because there is nothing else to do while they wait for death. Hamm claims he wants to be "finished," but admits that he "hesitate(s)" to do so. Beckett has compared Hamm and Clov's tense co-dependent relationship with his own relationship with his wife; each talked about leaving the other in the 1950s but was afraid to make the final move.

I was watching a woman on TV talk about her experiences of the emptiness and loneliness of life so well portrayed by Beckett, and she ended the interview with a story. She said that one day she was walking in the city and had to cross a road where the stoplight was red. As she waited she noticed in front of her a boy of about twelve, together with his grandmother, and when the light went to green, the boy walked backwards across the street, gazing and smiling at his grandmother and she at him. Witnessing that moment, the interviewee said, she knew what life was about.

Love *is* the only meaning, and the theater of the absurd is a waste of life.

The Tinker's Curse

By chance—or by design—I went to see a play called *The Tinker's Curse* in the most unlikely of venues—Bere Island in Bantry Bay, West Cork, in a large hut that is a vestige of British navy occupation. The author and actor of the one-man play, Michael Harding,* gave a superb, hour-long, intimate gaze into the life of a Tinker, or Traveler, as they are more usually called in Ireland.

The Tinker's monologue was interspersed with some pensive toot-ling on his flute and a few outbursts of rage at times when his feelings got the best of him and he was unable to speak. He—the author, ac-tor, traveler, mirror image of Irish men and women—was a wonderful storyteller and made us laugh a lot, but from the earliest moments he released whiffs of overwhelming sadness and longing about something the Tinker couldn't or didn't want to talk about. It was only minutes before the end of the play that he revealed his innermost secret. Why do most of us, whether we are travelers or apparently settled, wait a life-time or more to talk about it, when not to talk about the secret deprives us of feelings of joy and belonging and being at home with ourselves?

I am a traveler living in Ireland for a while in the place where my father was born. Like all Irishmen and many billions who are sure they have some Irish in them, I never wanted to talk about *it*. Living in this beautiful place, it quickly became apparent that the full-blooded Irish people don't want to talk about *it* either. They don't want to let anybody see into their inner sanctum, where their Mortality dwells and their supposed Mortal sins incubate guilt and shame. Furthermore, they don't want to let anybody—most particularly themselves—see into the centuries-old grief and sadness caused by death, famine, emigration,

---

*   Michael Harding, Livin' Dred Theatre, mhardingx@eircom.net

the Church, and the British, to name but a few. Come into the pub and we'll have a rare old time and maybe add a bit of singing and dancing to the occasion. But in the pub we don't have to go too deep, and we have an exit strategy.

I used to think it was just the men who dodged any expression of feelings other than anger, but it is the women too, for their readiness and skill in gossiping about what they imagine to be the actions and feelings of others is not to be mistaken for intimacy. I thought that men (my father, for example, and both of his sons) were terrified of the feminine, considering women as either virgins most-pure or, if sex was involved, lusty and all-engulfing whores. But it is not the feminine in women that causes such confusion and fear, but the feminine within each individual, man or woman.

Many or most of us squander much of our lives focusing on Mortal pursuits and ignore our feminine Soul that would provide love and witness and intimacy. We have too little of the feminine Soul in our lives, for the world has become increasingly masculine, with a Wildman Spirit powered more by violence and greed than by the energy and courage that would enable us to live loving lives.

In Ireland, I see and feel the Soul and Spirit of the beautiful people, but all of us behave even now as if it is a Mortal sin for us to live balanced lives in loving harmony, and this is a Tinker's Curse if ever there was one.

To Do or Not to Do

Doing is so easy. It is asking and receiving that many of us find difficult, though we may have little difficulty holding on to blows and buffets that we receive in many forms. Holding on to suffering is all too easy for many of us, and giving those same blows and buffets away or putting them down as a forgiving gesture may be the most difficult task in our lives.

To forgive is only a gaze away, and to ask for and receive the love we need is no further!

Soul on Ice

My Inner Being was frozen for half a century. Now, with inner global warming, the iceberg has melted and I am amazed and thrilled by the treasures exposed within, old and new.

Darkness

It is odd that the greater the circle of light we create, the less we may feel the need to gaze into the darkness from which all things are born.

Light and dark are adjacent bands in the spectrum, as inseparable as night and day. The art of living needs to include forays into the darkness, that we may bring back unexpected treasures into the light.

It is in the night that Soul and Spirit visit the sleeping Mortal, whispering in his ear the stuff of dreams and investing him with love and zest for living. Then he wakes refreshed and renewed, prepared to spread love around, having absorbed some of the energy of enlightenment.

Re-membering

We so quickly forget who we are and where we came from. We were born perfect, and we brought with us an Original Blessing as Mathew Fox averred, that I imagine to be a sign of celestial joy. Just gaze at the young child and gasp with delight and amazement as she shows us her three natures or members: Mortal, Soul, and Spirit. Her Mortal nature breathes with life and her Soul radiates love, and her Spirit kicks and waves with enthusiasm. She is complete, and she is "in" the state of love that exists when our three members are in balance. But not long after her birth she may forget one or other of her members and lose her balance as these natures become hidden or even erased by the Mortals around her.

If the child has the good fortune to have parents who love themselves and each other—if they are well prepared to be parents—her Soul and Spirit will flourish. But if Soul and Spirit are in partial or complete eclipse in the family, the child may lose sight of her own.

The Soul is the unconditional lover within the child, and it may withdraw. Perhaps her parents are fearful of gazing and being gazed at because they have not learned about loving themselves and feel vulnerable in the presence of the Soul of their child. When parents are afraid of showing their feelings, the child may learn to hide her own, and become out of touch with her Soul.

The Spirit is by nature a kind, energetic, collaborative and enthusiastic friend and lover of Mortals. If the child's parents are faint-hearted and uninspiring or if their behavior is aggressive and judgmental, the child's Spirit nature may not thrive. Timidity and unassertiveness may take the place of her liveliness and self-assertiveness, or her Spirit nature may take a darker, wilder, less collaborative form.

The market place for which most of us are prepared by our schooling has little place for the loving Soul and assertive Spirit, and when the goal of life in the competitive world is the accretion of what they define to be our "net worth," Soul and Spirit is eclipsed.

If we are to foster relationships with ourselves and others and live a loving life, we need to reunite—re-member—our three natures, and when we re-member them we will be "in" love once again, as it was in the beginning.

A Change of Life

Change is not easy, especially if we do not have the love and support of ourselves. Growing up, leaving home, emigration, marriage, death, and losses of all kinds—all upheavals require the inner power of love to keep our circulation flowing. In early childhood, I felt love and caring from my parents and to a lesser extent from God. The rules and regulations from Church and State appeared benign and all seemed well.

Then at the age of seven years, I was sent away to boarding school, and the warm blanket of love and care vanished, seldom to be sensed for the next fifty years. In those early years away from home I felt abandoned and dreadfully lonely, and was unable to draw on love and care from within. Even when I went home there was little comfort, because over the years I realized that my parents had never learned to love and care for themselves and each other. They lived in a constant fog of alcohol that made it impossible for them to love me or themselves unconditionally.

Church and State also revealed their loveless nature to me, as did medical school and a marriage like that of my parents. The problem for me was not "them." Yes, parents, priests, and potentates had all been taught little about love and so had little to offer me or anyone else, but I was never inspired to learn about loving myself until late in middle age, and was unable to give love to myself and receive it from others.

If we learn to love ourselves unconditionally with our inner Soul, and have confidence, enthusiasm, and support from our inner Spirit, all will be well. Changes, even the one from life to death, will be so much less fearful and painful, so let's not wait to learn about loving ourselves. Life is far too short to spend it in suffering!

Gazing at Death

A Japanese ceremony of preparing a corpse for cremation in the presence of the family and friends is the subject of *Departures,* a moving film that won the Oscar for the best foreign film in 2009.*

The ritual, performed by "encoffiners," is an art form of the greatest delicacy, providing the opportunity for the bereaved *to gaze uninterruptedly at death*. It is a reverential ceremony during which the family does nothing except gaze at the one who has died, and these sacred moments are a perfect prelude to letting go while retaining the inner knowledge and awareness of death.

Normally, we turn our eyes away from death. In the United States, the body is usually prepared by professionals in a chilly funeral "home" (away from home) for a brief glance or "viewing" that gives witnesses neither time nor place to absorb the reality of death and mortality. During the encoffinment ritual, the family is very much in the presence of death, fully in touch with mortality—their own, and that of their loved one.

I believe that this movie may inspire us to gaze at death and allow it to enter into our inner being. This antidote to denial gives death a distinct place within our inner consciousness and it becomes a little less fearful. In western funeral homes, and in the hustle and bustle of hospitals, there is neither time set aside nor any ritual that encourages and makes possible an extended gaze. I believe that if we will gaze at death in much the same way that we need to learn to gaze at life, we will develop a greater respect for life, and death will lose some of its sting by becoming more familiar and more of an undeniable part of the life of Mortals.

* *Departures,* directed by Yojiro Takito (available in DVD)

I Don't Want to Talk about It

Why dredge it up? Why revisit the pain and the terrors and the fear of death? Why go back to the Holocaust? Better to say it never happened, or to label it PTSD and give a pill, with the instructions that I think came from R.D. Laing:

Take this pill
It helps you not to shout.
It takes away the life
You're better off without.

The cost of not talking about it is that it festers deep within, unheard and untouched, and drains energy for living which requires witness and compassion if life is to be lived lovingly. So we *must* talk about it in words, but not necessarily with so very many words. The talk we need is mostly the silent act of gazing at ourselves with love and compassion, and also being witnessed and confirmed by others, for only then will the pain and terrors and fear of death dissolve.

It

It can happen in Ireland. As came to light in two thousand and nine, more than *eight hundred* adults physically and sexually abused many of the *one hundred and thirty thousand* defenseless children in over *two hundred* orphanages and educational or "corrective" institutions under the control of the "religious" during a period of thirty-five years— abuse that was both systematic and widely know about in high places, but ignored. Surely this can't be true, for this is Holy Ireland, remember. Breathtaking beauty and a hundred thousand welcomes on the one hand, with stormy weather and eons of religious madness on the other. When faced with the darker side of life, the conditioned response etched into our consciousness in Ireland—and in many other places—is "I don't want to talk about *it*," and this failure to talk becomes the defective system in which we live. If *it* should appear unbidden out of the darkness, the default system includes: "*It* is the will of God," or "Offer *it* up," or "Sure *it* can't be that bad" or the standby "Let's change the subject and have a drink."

What is *It* that we are so afraid of talking about? *It* is the silent Scream that the artist Edvard Munch depicted in his astonishing and disquieting painting. *It* is all the silent and not-so-silent screams from the Irish institutional hells-on-earth that were ignored, and there are still more such screams emanating from all manner of homes everywhere.

Mortality and death are also *it*, and to talk about mortality and death is usually considered morbid and unsocial or even ignorant and wrong in the face of imagined "eternal life" and "reincarnation" and other forms of institutional denial of the mortality of Mortals. Yes, we attend funerals in droves, but the silent screams of the mourners continue beyond the funeral, and those screams like the silent screams of our lost or lonely children are largely ignored, or the screamer is branded as being "depressed." With this label we can give a pill so that he or she can get on with *it*, but *it* will never go away until we ourselves acknowledge the pain and the terrors that are a part of *it*.

It is violence and death in all its forms. *It* is the suicide bombers and the perverted religious and political zealots everywhere that are a plague in our times as well as in times gone by. *It* is the biting "humor" of so many "comedians" and other malicious gossips that has become part of the defective system, and we call it "entertainment." *It* is the killer instinct that is so destructive of our planet and yet is believed to be essential to the conduct of business. However, *it* also destroys the bodies, Souls, and Spirits of many of the people conducting that business.

We *must* talk about *it*, for only then can we see that *it* is the absence of Love. We talk about love so often, but we usually confuse it with sex about which we talk endlessly. We may say that people who are having sex are "lovers" but that is often far from the truth, even in the institution of marriage. Love is simply the act of gazing gently and without any judgment at ourselves, first of all. We need to gaze deep into the mirror at the screamer who is abused or in mourning, without ordering the one in the mirror to forget *it*. Only when we remember *it* and gaze at *it* with love will the Scream disappear, and we will then have the energy to pass on the loving gaze to others. *It* will lose its force in the face of unconditional love, and when we love ourselves unconditionally we will have room to love others and not be obsessed with *it*.

So what we do need to talk about—and practice—is love and gazing with compassion, for only then will *it* become nothing to talk about.

Roots

Roots are tendrils that reach from the past into our inner being,
and provide a sense of connectedness to an infinite story
that has no room for loneliness.
As is the way in Inner Consciousnes,
the facts and details are of little importance,
for it is within the connectedness and freedom from judgment
that love dwells.

Laughter

When we forget how to laugh, we need to borrow a child and read a funny book to her. She will gaze with rapt attention at the flow of words, and ripples of infectious, unstoppable laughter will spill out from deep within. No canned hilarity here, or loud guffaws induced by humor that has its origins in mean-spiritedness. From the Soul of the child come bubbles of merriment that burst out loud, creating smiles and laugh wrinkles on the face of the reader that melt the ice of fear and sadness. Laughter is a homeopathic remedy for Mortal suffering that lubricates Mortals, preparing them to embrace the Soul and Spirit in everything.

The Grand Canyon

Huge beyond anything imaginable, its massive Spirit tattooed with colorful stripes. Vistas that thrill, bathed in sunlight that changes the scene from moment to moment. As I gaze at the wall of rock, the light softens, hardens, illuminates, and obscures, creating breathtaking moments of wonder and surprise

Gazing deep down, I saw a tiny venule in its bed of rock, short or a little longer depending on my point of view. This blue-white water carrier brings life to millions, and yet it is but a tiny strand within the beautiful layered rocks that contain evidence of war and peace, and of screams of anguish and cries of joy, while cradling the death masks of creatures great and small. The rocks hold volumes of history stacked one upon another, but it is the river that carries the moisture for life. The Colorado River might be imagined as the river of Love and Loss and Forgiveness, for it fosters life and love and offers cleansing absolution as it passes along. The river and the warmth of the sun and the shadows that wrap the rocks in their arms feel as if they are inhabited by the Soul of nature, and the majesty of multicolored rocks that attract our gaze appears to be a formidable manifestation of the Spirit of nature, offering strength and solace to the Soul. Mortals who simply look and photograph from the canyon rim with their Outer Awareness will miss the inner Soul and Spirit of the place, even if they get the picture.

Our inner life is like the Colorado, streaming through the unimaginable depths and heights of our being, with the ever-changing light at dawn and dusk inspiring Soul and Spirit, and the moments of illumination in between that causes Mortals to gasp with wonder at the ebb and flow of life. At night, everything vanishes into the darkness that is both prelude to a new day and a reminder to gazing Mortals that time is running out.

More Loneliness

My overly possessive mother (one of countless mothers who lavish affection on their children and neglect themselves, expecting that the child will give them the love that they fail to give themselves) was "standing in" for my Soul during childhood (as mothers and fathers need to do before the child "re-members" his own Soul and Spirit), and she then abandoned me to the terrors of loneliness in a far-off boarding school.

Mother did the same a few years later, when I found her unconscious and drunk on the floor and thought she was dead. This betrayal of an unspoken promise to always be there for me as a loving, witnessing Soul laid the foundation for loneliness that was not satisfied by marriage or children or professional success. When I was a child, I was unable to see that my mother was also a lonely Soul abandoned by coldly successful parents, and that she too never felt the warmth and comfort of her own Soul.

For some people, the notion of God provides the warmth and witness of Soul that we need, but for me as a child and young adult, that God was far too judgmental and I was far too steeped in guilt and shame for any solace to come from that direction.

It was not until I was past middle age and became able to gaze with love and compassion at the lonely Mortal in the mirror that I re-membered, and then my three natures became reunited. When my Mortal nature experienced the gaze of my Soul, together with the strength and enthusiasm of my Spirit, loneliness vanished. Now my three natures are one, and I am with me every day of my life till death do us part.

I never had an honest farewell with my mother till years after her death. Had I said goodbye, and asked for and given forgiveness, I might have been able to gaze in the mirror much earlier and found myself within rather than wasting so many years avoiding myself as well as her.

In Memoriam

Much of what we store in our memory
is the junk mail or spam of others
that has nothing to do with us.
Most obituaries are no different.

Mirror Mirror on the Wall

We often turn ourselves into someone who we dislike intensely because our parents or other important persons berated us so often that we began to believe we were the person they said we were. In rage and loathing and self-righteousness that they would probably deny, they called us useless or dumb or wild or mean or "a nobody." They may have assaulted us physically or sexually as well as emotionally, so that we began to live their image of who we were in excruciating detail. When we looked in the mirror, we detested the creation we saw.

What we could have seen in the mirror, if we had gazed long and deep enough, was sadness and the loss of innocence. A terrifying void was created by the absence of Soul and Spirit, for they fled from the abuse in times gone by, and we attempted to avoid that reflection at all costs by refusing to look.

It is the loss of self-esteem that we see in the mirror and it drives us mad, for we know that we cannot live lovingly without Soul and Spirit. It drives us mad with hatred or it drives us mad with grief, and we become depressed or filled with anxiety or, like Narcissus, we may kill ourselves. Psychiatrists give us diagnoses of depression or panic or anxiety and prescribe pills, but no pill has ever changed a reflection or filled a void.

Look again. Gaze softly, with the Soul's unconditional love, and ask forgiveness of the Mortal one in front of you for abandoning him, saying: "My dear one, please forgive me for not being there for you in those dreadful voids. From now on, I will be with you every day of your life, and at the time of your death I will hold you in my arms."

Leadership in the Face of Dragons, Warriors, and Other Dangers

How could we forget those ancient myths that stand at the beginning of all races, the myths about dragons that at the last moment are transformed into princesses? Perhaps all the dragons in our lives are princesses who are only waiting to see us act, just once, with beauty and courage. Perhaps everything that frightens us is, in its deepest essence, something helpless that wants our love. Rilke

Rage and fire and dragons may be transformed by the loving feminine into a masculine Spirit that protects and makes safe rather than one that conquers and kills. Young boys are often snatched too early from the maternal Soul that would have taught them softness. Instead, thrust into the arena of competition that judges them winners or losers, and admires terror-mongers that breathe fire and death, they learn to become warriors feted as heroes.

What causes us to make monsters out of men? All too often, warriors return home so very much alone and discover their brutalized Souls have forsaken them, causing love to pass them by. Many suffer from Post Traumatic Soul Destruction, and like Narcissus, some kill themselves. Others take pills and potions in a desperate attempt to fill the void.

Others, however, act with beauty and courage, and only in the face of beauty and courage will love reappear. For our survival, we need a new paradigm of masculine Spirit. We need a Spirit—a leader—who acts with beauty and courage and makes us safe for love. The age-old winner-warrior may promise security or survival and appear to be powerful, but this Spirit also creates legions of losers and coffins of the dead who will haunt us.

In the umbra of the disastrous and untrustworthy Presidential leadership of George W. Bush, we craved a new leadership that would inspire us to rise up and channel our energy into a powerhouse of love. We needed a hopeful and inspirational alternative to hunter-gatherer leaders or heroic warrior leaders, many of whom are violent Spirits from a dark side of history that still repeats itself to this day. We need not wait for the coming of a new political Spirit. We may adopt for ourselves a new paradigm of masculine Spirit that will love our feminine Soul, and our Mortal nature will feel safe and well prepared to live the loving life.

Then, and only then, will the world be transformed.

Storms at Sea

There is a huge storm churning the waves in southwest Ireland, where I am living as I write these words, and it seems like spring is blowing winter out to sea to make room for new beginnings.

Spring and Easter are special times to remind ourselves about love and loss and forgiveness. We often forget or neglect love and the shortness of our Mortal existence, as well as the need to let go of suffering in our lives.

I knew little about love in earlier years but was told that God loved me. Perhaps He or She did, but I certainly didn't. As I look back, I see myself surrounded by good people who often spoke about love but practiced self-neglect. I learned obediently from them, and love never became a part of me until much later in life. Like those in my proximity, I attempted to ignore most of my losses and all of my screams, and seldom if ever experienced loss as a catalyst for living a more *loving life*.

Without self-love, forgiveness was an impersonal ritual that passed me by, never releasing me from shame and guilt and self-neglect. But in later years, in hospice and in my workshops, I was fortunate to learn before it was too late.

The storm will pass, and in these opening moments of spring I will soon be part of a workshop in a beautiful monastery on the cliffs that I can see from my window a couple of miles away. For many of the participants there will be stormy sees within, and waves of feelings will be stirred up. But we will go through the turbulence together and be moved, and this rite of spring reminds us that there is no need to avoid the wild side within or without, for it is a necessary passage into the possibilities of summer.

Pause for a moment and gaze out to see. Can you hear the promise of spring from the far side of the wind?

Listen.

Imagine Loving Thy Neighbor as Thyself

We are urged to love our neighbors as ourselves, and it is a disaster for the neighbors. In fact, most of us hardly know our neighbors and probably don't like them, never mind love them. No big surprise, because many of us are also unfamiliar with ourselves. Loving ourselves is something that we have been lead to believe is weak or self-indulgent or narcissistic, regardless of the fact that Narcissus killed himself because he discovered that he was unable to love himself.

What if we really loved ourselves and then acted in the same manner towards those around us! Imagine waking up and saying to ourselves, "Good morning! How glad I am to see you!" Imagine being our own best friend, someone we can trust to whom we can take our concerns and worries without fear of judgment. Imagine being comfortable with solitude yet relishing connectedness!

Loving ourselves is giving voice to our feminine Soul nature. In our increasingly masculine world, the feminine within men is often unfamiliar. If as men we love ourselves or love other men, then we imagine we must be gay, regardless of the fact that sexual preference has little or nothing to do with love.

If we love ourselves, we might believe this to be a statement that we prefer self-love to a sexual relationship with another, regardless of the fact that masturbation and sexual relationships may have nothing to do with love: they may be more akin to scratching an itch than being expressions of love. If we feel love towards a woman other than our wife, that love is often seen as off limits because coveting our neighbor's wife is taboo, and it must mean that we want sex, regardless of the fact that we can love ourselves and others without sexual activity. So men are often lonely and out of touch with their feminine nature. They may only allow themselves sports talk, backslapping, and a variety of addictions and protective habits with men and flirtatious but not deeply penetrating exchanges with women.

For women and for men, loving ourselves is the best preparation for unconditionally loving others. Many women who have little love for themselves dedicate their lives to filling the feminine void in men. Filling the emptiness of another is impossible, as broken marriages and other relationships tell us, and neither the woman nor the man is satisfied once the bloom of sex is diminished.

So let's imagine loving ourselves. We will need to practice forgiveness; we will need to practice letting go of the doubts, judgments, and limitless ways in which we torture ourselves for not being someone else. Let's look in the mirror and love what we see. Let's meditate lovingly on ourselves, and when we feel fulfilled, the love will spill over and nourish others.

Alive!

In 1964, Robert Coles interviewed a poor black woman who spoke of the desperation of her life, and the difficulty of finding herself:

To me, having a baby inside me is the only time I'm really alive.

She was right and she always will be, for life is all about being pregnant. It is all about being alive and feeling alive with love inside, for that is what the inner child gives us. Yes, a woman feels alive during pregnancy, but if the life she feels is that of a child other than her self, the feeling will pass after she gives birth and not return until the next pregnancy.

It is only when we feel pregnant with love for ourselves that we feel really alive and know why Mona Lisa smiles. Women need to feel pregnant, and men need to feel pregnant. There is no other way of being in touch once again with our whole nature. There is no other way of remembering.

For men, making a killing during the hunting season or in the battlefield or in the stock market doesn't do it. Multiplying our net worth, or scoring with hoards of women, or being immersed in any other addiction does not fill the emptiness that only being pregnant and remembering will fill. Having a son and being filled with pride is no substitute for being pregnant with our own inner child and filled with love, for only when we are filled with love are we prepared to become lovers of our sons and peacemakers instead of warriors.

Let us all be aware and celebrate our lifelong pregnancy, for love is the only survival, the only meaning.

The Mortal: In Thanksgiving to the Dark Side

<u>Rage</u>
you served me well
when I was lost and filled with fear
and silent screams;
without your presence I would have vanished,
but now please leave me be
to live my life in love.

<u>Cigarettes</u>
companions and solace,
ever ready
in times of loneliness and stress,
but now I give you up with thanks
before my lungs expire.

<u>Alcohol</u>
always there in times of need
releasing tears and soothing fears,
you have my thanks and now
be off with you
before my mind and gut
are ruined
by your deadly charms.

Sex
up you came
and in I went
imagining
that to be in
was to be in love.
Now I know
that a gaze is prelude
to becoming
with no demand
to rise up

On Being Awake
Oh, Soul and Spirit
What need have I for aught but thee!